Short Stories for Students, Volume 5

Staff

Editorial: Tim Akers, Jerry Moore, *Editors*. Tim Akers, Joseph Alvarez, James Aren, Christine G. Berg, Thomas Bertonneau, Cynthia Bily, Yoonmee Chang, Carol Dell' Amico, Catherine Dominic, Catherine V. Donaldson, Tom Faulkner, Angela Frattarola, Tanya Gardiner-Scott, Terry Girard, Diane Andrews Henningfeld, Richard Henry, Erik Huber, Kendall Johnson, Dustie Kellet, David Kippen, Rena Korb, Ondine Le Blanc, Jean Leverich, Sarah Madsen Hardy, Thomas March, Jerry Moore, Carl Mowery, Robert Peltier, Jane Phillips, Elisabeth Piedmont-Marton, Shaun Strohmer, *Sketchwriters*. Jeffrey W. Hunter, Daniel Jones, John D. Jorgenson, Deborah A. Schmitt, Polly Vedder, Timothy J. White, Kathleen Wilson, *Contributing Editors*. James P. Draper, *Managing Editor*.

Research: Victoria B. Cariappa, *Research Team*

Manager. Andrew Malonis, *Research Specialist.*

Permissions: Susan M. Trosky, *Permissions Manager.* Kimberly Smilay, *Permissions Specialist.* Kelly Quin, *Permissions Associate.*

Production: Mary Beth Trimper, *Production Director.* Evi Seoud, *Assistant Production Manager.* Shanna Heilveil, *Production Assistant.*

Graphic Services: Randy Bassett, *Image Database Supervisor.* Mikal Ansari, Robert Duncan, *Imaging Specialists.* Pamela A. Reed, *Photography Coordinator.*

Copyright Notice

Copyright 1999
The Gale Group
27500 Drake Road
Farmington Hills, MI 48331-3535

This book is printed on acid-free paper that meets the minimum requirements of American National Standard for Information Sciences—Permanence Paper for Printed Library Materials, ANSI Z39.48-1984.

ISBN 0-7876-2220-6
ISSN 1092-7735

Printed in the United States of America
10 9 8 7 6 5 4 3 2

Recitatif

Toni Morrison 1983

Introduction

"Recitatif" is the only published short story by luminary African-American novelist Toni Morrison. It appeared in a 1983 anthology of writing by African-American women entitled *Confirmation,* edited by Amiri and Amina Baraka. "Recitatif" tells the story of the conflicted friendship between two girls—one black and one white—from the time they meet and bond at age eight while staying at an orphanage through their re-acquaintance as mothers on different sides of economic, political, and racial divides in a recently gentrified town in upstate New York.

While Morrison typically writes about black

communities from an inside perspective, in this story she takes a different approach. The story explores how the relationship between the two main characters is shaped by their racial difference. Morrison does not, however, disclose which character is white and which is black. Rather than delving into the distinctive culture of African Americans, she illustrates how the divide between the races in American culture at large is dependent on blacks and whites defining themselves in opposition to one another. Her use of description and characterization in the story underscores the readers' complicity in this process. Morrison has considered similar issues in her book of criticism, *Playing in the Dark: Whiteness and the Literary Imagination,* which explores how language enforces stereotypes in the work of classic American authors such as Melville, Poe, and Hemingway. "Recitatif" may therefore be understood as part of Morrison's ongoing response to the mostly white and male classic literary tradition of the United States.

Author Biography

Toni Morrison was born Chloe Anthony Wofford to George and Rahmah Wofford in 1931. The second of four children, Morrison was raised in the small Ohio town of Lorain in a tight-knit black community. Morrison describes her father, a shipyard welder, as a racist. Having experienced virulent racism, he despised whites. Her mother, on the other hand, was an integrationist. Both of her parents and her larger community instilled in Morrison a strong sense of self-esteem and cultural identity.

Though she had no aspirations of being a writer in her youth, Morrison was always an avid reader and a precocious student. Her imagination was further nourished by the folk stories passed down from her parents and grandmother. She attended Lorain High School and went on to Howard University, a historically black college. There she studied English and drama and came to be known as Toni. In 1955 Morrison earned a master's degree in English from Cornell University and began a teaching career. She married Harold Morrison, a Jamaican architect, and they had two sons, Harold and Slade.

Morrison's writing career began at age 30 when, feeling unfulfilled, she joined an informal writer's group. Morrison drafted a short story about a black girl who wished she had blue eyes. She had never written fiction or poetry before. This story was the seed of her first novel, *The Bluest Eye,* which she published nine years later. In the interim, Morrison divorced her husband and left teaching, moving to New York for a career in editing. As an editor at Random House she fostered the careers of some of the most important black female writers of her generation. After the appearance of *The Bluest Eye* in 1970, Morrison continued to write prolifically, with great popular and critical success. She is the author of seven novels, a play, and a work of literary criticism. "Recititaf" is her only published work of short fiction. Since 1987 she has focused mainly on writing but has also taught classes at Yale and Princeton Universities.

Morrison is one of the most loved and respected writers of the late twentieth century. Several of her books have been bestsellers and she is the recipient of a number of prestigious literary awards. In 1993 Morrison was awarded the Nobel Prize for Literature, becoming the first African American to win this honor.

The story opens with a description of "St. Bonny's" or St. Bonaventure, the shelter where Twyla, the narrator, meets Roberta, the story's other main character, when they are both eight years old. Twyla recalls that her mother once told her that people of Roberta's race smell funny, and she objects to being placed in a room with Roberta on the grounds that her mother wouldn't approve. Twyla, however, soon finds Roberta understanding and sympathetic to her situation. While most children at the shelter are orphans, Twyla is there because her mother "dances all night" and Roberta is there because her mother is sick. Roberta and Twyla are isolated from the other children at St. Bonny's and are scared of the older girls, so they stick together.

Twyla remembers St. Bonny's orchard in particular but she doesn't know why it stands out in her memory. She recounts an incident in which Maggie, a mute woman who worked at St. Bonny's kitchen, fell down in the orchard and the big girls laughed at her. Twyla reports that she and Roberta did nothing to help her. They called her names and she ignored them, perhaps because she was deaf, but Twyla thinks not and, looking back, she is ashamed.

Twyla and Roberta's mother come to visit one Sunday. The girls are excited and get dressed up to meet them at church services. Twyla is embarrassed by Mary, her mother, because of her casual appearance, but also proud that she is so pretty. When Roberta attempts to introduce her mother to Twyla and Mary, her mother refuses to address them or to shake Mary's extended hand, presumably because of racial prejudice. Mary says "That bitch!" right there in the chapel and further embarrasses Twyla by groaning during the service. Roberta's mother wears a huge cross and carries a large Bible. Afterward, Mary and Twyla eat Easter candy, since Mary has brought no lunch for them, while Roberta can't finish the food her mother brought. Not long after, Roberta leaves St. Bonny's.

Twyla doesn't see Roberta again for many years. Twyla is now a waitress, and Roberta comes in to the Howard Johnson's where she works. Roberta is with two men and tells Twyla that they are on their way to see Jimi Hendrix, but Twyla doesn't know who Hendrix is. Roberta dismisses Twyla and calls her an asshole. Twyla responds by asking about Roberta's mother and cattily reports that her own is still "pretty as a picture."

Tywla's narration picks up again when she is 28 years old and married. She describes her home, husband, and family life. Newburgh, the rundown town where they live, has recently become gentrified, and there is a new mall at the edge of town where Twyla goes one day to shop at a gourmet supermarket. There she runs into Roberta, now married to a wealthy executive, for the first time since their hostile encounter at Howard Johnson's. Roberta greets Twyla warmly and asks her to a coffee. They laugh and the tension between them seems to dissolve. As they are reminiscing, the incident with Maggie comes up. Roberta claims that Maggie didn't fall down in the orchard, but that the big girls had knocked her down. This is not what Twyla remembers and she starts to feel uncomfortable. She asks Roberta about their encounter at Howard Johnson's and Roberta answers, "Oh, Twyla, you know how it was in those days: black-white." They part ways, promising to keep in touch.

That fall racial tension descends on Newburgh as a result of busing, instituted to ensure integration in the schools. Twyla's son Joseph is one of the children who has to take a bus to a school in a different area. Twyla is driving near the school Joseph will attend and sees Roberta picketing against busing. Twyla stops and they discuss the issue. They argue and soon the group of picketers surrounds Twyla's car and start rocking it; Twyla reaches out to Roberta for help, but Roberta does nothing. Police finally come to Twyla's aid. Just before she pulls away, Roberta approaches her and calls her "the same little state kid who kicked a poor old black lady when she was down on the ground." Twyla responds that Maggie wasn't black and that Roberta is a liar. Roberta responds that she is the liar and that they had both kicked Maggie.

Twyla begins to stand on a picket line holding up slogans that respond directly to Roberta's. Over the course of the six weeks that the schools are closed due to the controversy, Twyla's signs become more personal, with slogans like, "Is your mother well?"

Twyla and Roberta have no interactions for a long time, but Twyla remains preoccupied with what Roberta said about Maggie. She knows that she didn't kick her, but she is perplexed about the question of whether the "sandy-colored" woman might have been black. One night she runs into Roberta, who is coming out of an elegant party at a downtown hotel. She approaches Twyla and says she has something she has to tell her. She admits that they had never kicked Maggie but says that she really did think that she was black. She confesses to having wanted to kick her and "wanting to is doing it." Roberta's eyes fill up with tears. Twyla thanks her and tells her, "My mother, she never did stop dancing." Roberta answers that hers never got well and begins to cry hard, asking "What the hell happened to Maggie?"

Characters

James Benson

James Benson is Twyla's husband. He is a native of Newburgh, the town where the later part of the story takes place. He is "comfortable as a house slipper" and is associated with the kind of family and continuity that Twyla's history lacks.

Joseph Benson

Joseph Benson is Twyla and James's son. Twyla becomes an activist in the busing controversy when Joseph is bused out of district in order to ensure racial integration in the schools.

Twyla Benson

Twyla is the main character and the story's narrator. She was raised, in part, at an orphanage—not because her parents were dead, but because her mother chose or needed to "dance all night" and was thus unable to care for her. The fact that Twyla lacks mothering is central to her character. She marries into a stable, rooted family and becomes a mother herself. It is in this capacity that she becomes involved in the controversy over racial integration in the schools and gets into a conflict with Roberta, a friend from the orphanage with whom she has recently become reacquainted.

Twyla is characterized throughout the story in terms of her relationship to Roberta, which is often one of contrast. As in their divide over the busing crisis, these contrasts are based around the central issue of their racial difference. Despite the fact that Twyla and Roberta are of different races and also, as the story progresses, different economic classes, there are underlying similarities and shared experiences—particularly their relationships to their respective mothers—that suggest the possibility of understanding and friendship. However, the events of the story illustrate that this possibility is precarious due to the social and cultural pressures that discourage interracial friendship.

Big Bozo

Big Bozo is the nickname for Mrs. Itkin, who oversees the care of Twyla and Roberta while they stay at St. Bonny's shelter. Although she is their caretaker, she is not warm or maternal. The girls are allied in their dislike for Big Bozo.

Roberta Fisk

Roberta is Twyla's friend and she is also the source of the main conflict of the story. The two girls meet while they are staying at an orphanage, though both of their mothers are living. Roberta's mother is a stern, religious woman who is too sick to care for her. The fact that both girls have mothers who are unable to care for them is central to their connection and sympathy. Despite this bond, their racial difference causes the friendship to founder. Roberta snubs Twyla the first time they see each other years after leaving the orphanage. She is warm to her the next time they meet, after another twelve years have passed and Roberta has married a wealthy executive. But now that both Roberta and Twyla are themselves mothers, their racially determined opposition is exhibited through their different positions in the busing controversy that takes over their town. Their conflict is further symbolized through their differing memories of Maggie, a racially ambiguous mute woman who worked at the orphanage.

Mrs. Itkin

See Big Bozo

Maggie

Maggie works at the kitchen of St. Bonny's, the orphanage where Twyla and Roberta meet. She is mute and bowlegged and was herself raised in an institution. One of Twyla's strongest memories of St. Bonny's is an incident where Maggie fell down in the school's orchard. Twyla remembers the intimidating older girls from the orphanage laughing at Maggie and that she and Roberta did nothing to help her. But during their argument over the busing controversy Roberta tells Twyla that they had both kicked Maggie that day, and further confuses her by referring to Maggie as a black lady. Twyla had never considered Maggie black. Roberta later admits that they had not kicked her, only that she had wanted to. But both women remain confused as to what race "sandy-colored" Maggie should be considered. Twyla and Roberta identify with Maggie's weakness and also identify her with their mothers, and both regard her with a combination of sympathy and anger.

Mary

Mary is Twyla's mother. Twyla has to stay at St. Bonny's because Mary cannot take care of her. According to Twyla, this is due to the fact that Mary "danced all night." Mary is pretty and affectionate but she is an irresponsible and neglectful mother. She is contrasted to Roberta's mother, who is large, stern, and judgmental.

Roberta Norton

See Roberta Fisk

Roberta's mother

Roberta has to stay at St. Bonny's because her mother is too sick to take care of her. Roberta's mother wears a huge cross and carries a huge Bible. She brings Roberta plenty of good food but is not warm and refuses to shake hands with Mary.

Race and Racism

The issue of race and racism is central to the story. Twyla's first response to rooming with Roberta at St. Bonny's is to feel sick to her stomach. "It was one thing to be taken out of your own bed early in the morning—it was something else to be stuck in a strange place with a girl from a whole other race." Throughout the story Twyla and Roberta's friendship is inhibited by this sense of an uncrossable racial divide, played out against the background of national racial tensions such as the busing crisis. Racial conflicts provide the main turning points in the story's plot. At no point, however, does Morrison disclose which girl is black and which is white. She offers socially and historically specific descriptions in order to flesh out her characterizations of Twyla and Roberta, and some of these descriptions may lead readers to come to conclusions about the characters" races based on associations, but none is definitive. For example, when Roberta shows up at the Howard Johnson's where Twyla works, on her way to see Jimi Hendrix, she's described as having "hair so big and wild I could hardly see her face." This may *suggest* that Roberta is black and wore an afro, a style for black hair popular in the 1960s. During this same period, however, hair and clothing styles (and music such as that of black rocker Hendrix) crossed over between black and white youths, and many whites wore their hair big and wild. Likewise, Roberta's socioeconomic progress from an illiterate foster care child to a rich executive's wife may *suggest* that she is white because of the greater economic power of whites in general. In Twyla's words, "Everything is so easy for them." Although economic class can be associated with race, there are plenty of white firemen and black executives. Race divides Twyla and Roberta again and again, and Morrison's unconventional approach to character description suggests that it is the way that blacks and whites are defined (and define themselves) against each other that leads to this divide.

Topics for Further Study

- Morrison intentionally withholds an important piece of information about Twyla and Roberta. Their racial difference is pivotal to the story, but readers don't know which one is white and which is black. How does this affect your experience of reading and your approach to interpreting the story? Find another example where an author withholds significant information about the characters or events of his or her story. Does the strategy have a similar or different effect in this case?

- Many readers may have come to conclusions about Twyla and Roberta's race based on descriptions Morrison offers of their situations and characteristics. List the "clues" or "codes" of race from the text that led you to your conclusion. What kinds of descriptions seem to suggest racial categories indirectly? Then look at the story again and see if you can find evidence to make the opposite argument.

- Maggie, the mute kitchen woman, is central to Twyla and Roberta's memories of St. Bonny's and to their relationship to one another. Each makes a different assumption about Maggie's race. Why is Maggie so important and what is the significance of whether she is black or white? Find some information about how racial categories are defined in the United States in contrast to other countries. How does this help you interpret the significance of Maggie's racial designation in the story?

- The story is set over a period of more than 20 years, between the late 1950s and early 1980s. Decide which section of the story interests you most and research American race relations during the decade in which it takes place. How does the story's historical context enrich your understanding of Twyla and Roberta's relationship?

- American literature offers many examples of interracial friendships, though these friendships are often compromised by unequal power relations. Think of an example of such a friendship from one of the classics of American literature that you are already familiar with. How are the themes of Morrison's story similar or different? Can you imagine how Morrison's story might be understood as a response or an answer to the classic example?

Difference

While Morrison uses the device of withholding information about the characters' races in order to make a specific point about black-white relations in the mid-twentieth century, it also works to make a more general point about how differences among people are understood. Though there are people of many races living in the United States and even many people of mixed racial background, race is often understood in terms of a black-white difference. Because readers don't know which character is black and which is white, they are challenged to consider the way that these labels are created out of various opposing sets of associations or social codes. At one point Twyla comments on her protest sign slogan, admitting that "actually my sign didn't make sense without Roberta's." This may be understood as a metaphor for the idea of difference that Morrison expresses in the story. The signs or codes used to suggest Twyla's race don't make sense without an opposing set of signs or codes that define Roberta in contrast.

Friendship

Twyla and Roberta's relationship gives shape to the plot of the story, which traces their interactions over more than twenty years. The story explores the possibilities and the failures of their friendship. The first sentence of "Recitatif," "My mother danced all night and Roberta's was sick," establishes that Twyla and Roberta's situations are parallel on the one hand, yet opposite on the other. It is this quality that makes friendship between the girls such a complicated prospect. While Twyla's mother is healthy and attractive, but immoral, Roberta's is sick and unattractive, but upstanding. Twyla's mother has cautioned her against people of Roberta's race, saying they smell funny, and Roberta's mother refuses to shake Twyla's mother's hand. Nevertheless, the girls share the scarring experience of having been left in an orphanage by their living mothers, and their feelings of abandonment allow them an implicit sympathy and sense of alliance. Throughout the story the women's situations mirror each other, with certain correspondences bringing them together and suggesting the potential for a deep and genuine friendship, but with just as many differences causing conflict, distrust, and resentment. The end of the story suggests some degree of reconciliation, but the possibility of enduring friendship is still tenuous.

Point of View

Twyla is the main character and also the narrator of the story. She describes the events in the first person, from her own perspective, and the events are presented as Twyla remembers them. One of the places where point of view is most pivotal is in terms of memories of Maggie. Early in the story, Twyla describes her memories of the orchard. At first she claims that "nothing really happened there. Nothing all that important, I mean," then goes on to describe how one day the orphanage's mute kitchen women, Maggie, fell down in the orchard and the big girls laughed at her. But as the story progresses it becomes clearer and clearer that this event was very significant to both Twyla and Roberta and to their relationship with one another. Twyla's memories of the incident are challenged when Roberta reports first that the big girls had pushed Maggie down, and then later not only that the two of them had joined in and kicked her, but that Maggie was black. Since Roberta had shared with Twyla this important and formative time at the orphanage, her differing recollections shake Twyla's confidence in her own ability to remember accurately, but also feed her existing distrust of Roberta.

Characterization

Morrison has an unusual approach to describing her characters. Though from the outset it is clear that Roberta and Twyla are of different races, Morrison does not disclose which girl is black and which is white. She does, however, offer rich and subtle descriptions of their ideas about racially sensitive issues, their social and economic status, their behavior, and their appearances. In this way, Morrison challenges readers to analyze their own assumptions about how these qualities may or may not be related to blackness and whiteness.

Plot

The story takes place over a period of more than 20 years, from the late 1950s when both girls are staying at St. Bonny's, through the early 1980s when their children have graduated from high school. The particular events of the story are played out against the historical setting of the mid-twentieth century. In particular, they span the most crucial years of the Civil Rights Movement, at times corresponding directly with specific events important to the Movement. For example, when Twyla and Roberta meet in the Howard Johnson's, Twyla mentions that students are riding buses South as activists for integration. Later, the women come into conflict over the controversial school integration tactic of busing. At times the history of race relations is reflected more indirectly, as in the assumptions about segregation at St. Bonny's.

The story is structured by Twyla and Roberta's sporadic interactions over this long period. Each of their meetings is described in detail, while important events in the narrator's life such as her marriage are barely mentioned. The plot is further shaped by the two women's conversations about and disagreements over the event in the orchard with Maggie. This seemingly trivial event is reevaluated almost every time Twyla and Roberta speak, and its significance resonates symbolically through the other plot conflicts up to the story's conclusion.

Symbolism

The style of the story is realistic and its symbolism is understated. Food, for example, recurs throughout the plot and is symbolic of the motif of mothering, nurturing, and abandonment. At St. Bonny's Roberta gives Twyla her extra food, symbolizing the symbiotic alliance between the girls. Later, when her mother visits, Twyla spills her candy on the floor, and later this is what they eat for lunch. Twyla's mother does not understand what her daughter needs, so Twyla is literally as well as symbolically undernourished. Twyla reports that "the wrong food is always with the wrong people. Maybe that's why I got into waitress work later—to match up the right people with the right food." Not only is food symbolic of mothering and the lack thereof, it is also more generally symbolic of the unfair or unequal ways that sustaining resources are distributed. In this light, it is significant that the despised and pitied figure of Maggie is employed at the orphanage as a kitchen woman. Both Twyla and Roberta associate her with their mothers' shortcomings in offering them care, and also with their own capacity for unfairness and disloyalty.

Race Relations in the 1950s: Segregation

In the 1950s communities throughout the country, particularly in the South, had segregated public facilities, including schools, public transportation, and restaurants. Throughout the country, social and cultural segregation was the norm. There were several landmark events in the struggle for racial equality during this decade and it is considered to mark the beginning of the Civil Rights Movement. In 1954, overturning a 1896 decision, the Supreme Court ruled that segregated schools were unconstitutional, though integration would occur gradually. The decision was met with strong resistance from politicians and the public alike. The state government of Arkansas defied the Supreme Court and attempted to prevent black children from entering and integrating the Little Rock public schools. Blacks became organized around other forms of segregation as well. In 1956 Rosa Parks, a middle-aged seamstress, refused to give up her seat on a Birmingham, Alabama, bus for a white commuter, igniting a year-long bus boycott. Martin Luther King, Jr., emerged as the leader of the movement.

Race Relations in the 1960s: Civil

Rights Activism

Blacks began to stage "sit-ins" at white lunch counters and restaurants across the South in protest of segregation. Northern students, radicalized by their opposition to the Vietnam War, joined the Civil Rights Movement in greater numbers, participating in marches and voter registration drives. More middle-class whites became enamoured of black culture and more blacks became aware of their African roots. Organized demonstrations were planned, with both black and white student activists participating in "freedom rides" to the South in protest of segregated interstate public transportation policies. Martin Luther King rose to national prominence, promoting a philosophy of nonviolence. A number of activists, both black and white, were killed as a result of their positions, and King himself was assassinated in 1968. King's death led to intense disillusionment among many, followed by greater divisiveness among activists, the rise of Black Power separatism, and renunciation in some quarters of the nonviolent approach.

Race Relations in the 1970s: Busing

While much of the racial conflict of the 1960s took place in the South, Northern cities became more of a flashpoint in the Civil Rights strife of the 1970s. Economic strain and police brutality contributed to race riots in a number of cities, which alienated some white activists. One of the most significant triggers to racial tension in the North was the institution of busing to ensure the desegregation of schools. 1971 marked the beginning of court-ordered school busing. Courts declared that "de facto" segregation existed in many northern urban school districts and found it to be illegal. This meant that the courts found Northern schools to be effectively segregated due to the existing racial mix in many school districts and neighborhoods, and that children must be bused out of their neighborhoods in order to ensure a fair access to educational resources. Busing ignited protests and outbreaks of violence in many communities. In the same time period, many blacks began to benefit from more equitable laws, entering politics and other positions of power in unprecedented numbers.

Critical Overview

"Recitatif" was published in a 1983 anthology of writings by African-American women entitled *Confirmation*. The purpose of the anthology—edited by Amiri Baraka, one of the most prominent voices of the radical Black Arts Movement of the 1960s, and his wife Amina—was to confirm the existence of several generations of black female writers whose work was often ignored or undervalued. Baraka writes in his introduction that the intention of the anthology is "in distinct contrast to the norm in American letters where 'American literature' is for the most part white and male and bourgeois." This is in keeping with Morrison's view of her mission as a writer. Saying that she is foremost a reader, she claims that she writes the kind of books that she wants to read but hasn't been able to find.

Compare & Contrast

- **1950s:** Most children whose parents have died or who cannot care for them live in institutions. Orphanage care has been in decline, however, in the United States since the end of World War II.

  1990s: Institutional care has fallen out of favor among childcare experts. Though they still exist in some places, orphanages have not been an important factor in child welfare in the United States for a decade. Foster care or support for continued care within the family is preferred.

- **1950s:** In 1954 the Supreme Court rules that segregation by race in public schools is unconstitutional. Black and white children begin to attend the same schools for the first time in many communities. The new law meets fierce opposition. In 1958 the governor of Arkansas calls for the Little Rock schools to be closed rather than integrated.

1970s: Courts find that "de-facto" school segregation—caused by segregated neighborhoods and school districts rather than intentionally segregated schools—is illegal. In segregated communities across the country courts order crosstown busing to ensure racial integration in public schools. In many cases this leads to protest and outbreaks of violence.

1990s: There is a loss of support for busing among African Americans due to the fact that it has failed to close the gap in academic achievement between black and white students. Courts overturn decisions to desegregate schools by means of busing in favor of more flexible measures such as charter and magnet schools. One study shows that students are one-sixth as likely to choose a friend of a different race than one of their own race.

- **1970s:** In the wake of a 1967 ruling that declared state laws banning interracial marriage to be unconstitutional, interracial relationships, marriage, and offspring become more prevalent.
  1990s: The number of interracial marriages has tripled since 1967 and there are over a million biracial families. In 1990 the category "other" is added to the five existing racial categories on the U.S. Census. In 1997 there is a movement to replace "other" with a biracial or multiracial category.

- **1970s:** The phenomenon of gentrification—in which high-income professionals move into rundown neighborhoods and renovate deteriorating buildings—becomes a housing trend. Gentrification results in the rebirth of old neighborhoods but also the displacement of low-income residents.

1990s: Gentrification, which was rampant throughout the 1980s, has slowed, but the displacement of poorer residents is still an issue in many neighborhoods.

The *Confirmation* anthology marked the beginning of a period when an unprecedented number of black women writers—Alice Walker, Jamaica Kincaid, Gloria Naylor, and Morrison among them—rose to prominence and "crossed over" for commercial success among a mostly white reading public. While Morrison had already published several notable novels by 1983, including *Song of Solomon,* which won the National Book Critics Circle Award and is considered to have signaled her status as an author of the first ranks, she had not yet reached her present level of distinction. She is now considered not only the foremost African-American woman writer but among the foremost living writers of any nation, race, or gender.

Morrison's greatest fame came with the publication of 1987's *Beloved.* When this emotionally-gripping and tragic story of an ex-slave and the daughter she murdered failed to win any major American prizes, a group of prominent black writers and intellectuals published a letter of protest in the *New York Times Book Review* decrying the lack of national attention to her work. *Beloved* won the Pulitzer Prize for Fiction the following year and contributed to Morrison's selection in 1993 as the recipient for the Nobel Prize in Literature, the world's highest literary honor. In addition to profuse critical and scholarly praise, many of Morrison's novels have been bestsellers. In 1992 Morrison published a novel and a work of criticism which were on the fiction and non-fiction bestseller lists simultaneously.

Morrison's precipitous rise and her mastery of the novel form have perhaps overshadowed her other achievements. Though she has written a play and a book of criticism, Morrison is known first and foremost as a novelist. 'Recitatif is Toni Morrison's only published work of short fiction and the story has received little critical attention, especially when compared to the huge amount of scholarship concerning Morrison's major novels. It differs significantly from her novels aesthetically, for it lacks the dimension of magic that has led critics to compare her writing to the Latin American school of magical realism. It shares, however, with her principal works a concern with history, memory, and the power of naming within the racial culture of the United States.

In an interview with Elissa Schappell for the *Paris Review* Morrison explains that her objective as a black writer in a white-dominated culture is to attempt to "alter language, simply free it up, not to repress it or confine it, but to open it up. Tease it. Blast its racist straightjacket." This is her intention in not naming the races of the two women in

"Recitatif." Morrison admits that she intended to confuse the reader, but also to "provoke and enlighten. . . . What was exciting was to be forced as a writer not to be lazy and rely on obvious codes." Commenting on this strategy, critic Jan Furman writes in *Toni Morrison's Fiction* that, like Twyla and Roberta, readers experience a disillusionment or dystopia, "if one may view Morrison's deliberate and clever misappropriation of racial stereotype as a dystopic condition for readers accustomed to stereotypes. In 'Recitatif' racial identities are shifting and elusive. . . . Questions beget questions in Morrison's text, and all require strenuous consideration. Despite most readers" wishes to assess, settle, draw conclusions, Morrison is resolute in requiring readers to participate in creating meaning." Such participation is characteristic of Morrison's goal as a writer to transform readers through transforming their relationship to language. In his introduction to *Toni Morrison: Critical Perspectives Past and Present* Henry Louis Gates, Jr., aptly describes the power of Morrison's writing as lying in the fact that it is "at once difficult and popular. A subtle craftsperson and a compelling weaver of tales, she 'tells a good story," but the stories she tells are not calculated to please."

What Do I Read Next?

- *Common Ground: A Turbulent Decade in the Lives of Three American Families* (1985) is an engaging history of the busing crisis in Boston written by J. Anthony Lukas. Focusing on three typical families who have very different relationships to the controversy, Lukas shows the complicated politics of the situation and also allows the readers to feel for those with whom they may disagree.

- *The Bluest Eye* (1970), Toni Morrison's first novel, tells the story of a young black girl growing up in Depression-era Ohio who believes that if she had blue eyes she would be happy. Morrison explores themes of beauty and self respect in a white-dominated culture.

- *Song of Solomon* (1977), another novel by Toni Morrison, traces a young man's struggle for cultural identity against the backdrop of a tragic and magical family history and the shifting racial climate of the mid-twentieth century. This novel won the National Book Critics Circle Award and was chosen for Oprah Winfrey's book club.

- *The Content of Our Character: A New Vision of Race in America* (1990) is academic Shelby Steele's collection of controversial and introspective essays on race relations in the wake of affirmative action. Steele combines personal experience and social psychology in his exploration of this hot topic.

- *Meridian* (1976), a novel by Alice Walker, dramatizes the ideas and experiences of the Civil Rights Movement through a Southern black activist named Meridian. Through this heroic woman the drama and conflict of this chapter of American history are brought to life.

- *Black-Eyed Susans and Midnight Birds* (1990), edited by Mary Helen Washington, is an anthology of black women's writing since 1960. It collects twenty stories by the most important and respected black women authors of our day.

Sources

Baraka, Amiri. Introduction to *Confirmation: An Anthology of African American Women,* New York: Quill, 1983.

Furman, Jan. *Toni Morrison's Fiction,* Columbia: University of South Carolina Press, 1996.

Gates, Henry Louis, Jr. Introduction to *Toni Morrison: Critical Perspectives Past and Present,* New York: Amistad, 1993.

Schappell, Elissa. Interview with Toni Morrison in *The Paris Review,* Vol. 35, No. 128, Fall, 1993, pp. 82-125.

Further Reading

Gates, Henry Louis, Jr., and K. A. Appiah, eds. *Toni Morrison: Critical Perspectives Past and Present,* New York: Amistad, 1993.

> An extensive collection of reviews and literary critical analyses of Morrison's work from many of the foremost scholars of African-American literature.

Jordan, Winthrop. *White Man's Burden: The Historical Origins of Racism in the United States,* New York: Oxford University Press, 1974.

> This short but sophisticated book explores how the idea of race and racial difference took root in the United States and formatively shaped national history.

Taylor-Guthrie, Danille, ed. *Conversations with Toni Morrison,* Jackson: University Press of Mississippi, 1994.

> In this collection of previously published interviews Morrison discusses many aspects of her life and work, as well as racial politics and American and African-American literary traditions.

Lightning Source UK Ltd.
Milton Keynes UK
UKOW01f1350231017
311496UK00006B/885/P

9 781375 386876